I AM!

FUN & INTERESTING

FACTS ABOUT

GIRLS

"From Childhood to Adulthood"

By MICHELLIAH MCCRANEY

I Am! Fun and Interesting Facts about Girls from Childhood to Adulthood
Copyright © 2018 by Michelliah McCraney

ISBN: 978-0998101354

Empyrion Publishing
PO Box 784327
Winter Garden FL 34778
Info@EmpyrionPublishing.com

Photo credits:
Page 1, 2 & 21 ~ Olillia©123rf.com

Page 5 ~ len44ik©123rf.com

Page 8 ~ sjhuls©123rf.com, pat138241©123rf.com, wavebreakmediamicro©123rf.com

pyotr©123rf.com, sam74100©123rf.com, stockbroker©123rf.com

Page 13 ~ arleevector©123rf.com

Page 14 ~ vector17©123rf.com, stockbroker©123rf.com, annettbro©123rf.com

desertsolitaire©123rf.com

Page 18 ~ leolintang©123rf.com

Page 23 ~ kakigori©123rf.com

Page 29 ~ sam74100©123rf.com

Page 30 ~ ferli©123rf.com

Page 31 ~ wavebreakmediamicro©123rf.com

Page 33 ~ hanaschwarz©123rf.com

Back Cover ~ michauljung©123rf.com, franckito©123rf.com,

studiograndouest©123rf.com, rocketclips©123rf.com

Printed in the United States of America.

I AM!

Educating! Equipping! & Empowering! Girls

From Childhood to Adulthood

Elementary, high school, college, careers, becoming a mother, marriage, and more

I AM! Series by Michelliah McCraney
I AM! EVERY GIRL NEEDS TO KNOW WHO SHE IS
I AM! 10 TRUTHS TO HELP GIRLS KNOW WHO THEY ARE
I AM! FUN AND INTERESTING FACTS ABOUT GIRLS FROM
CHILDHOOD TO ADULTHOOD
and
I AM! ALL-IN-ONE WORKBOOK AND JOURNAL

Being an educator, mother and grandmother I know the importance of girls knowing their strength and being empowered to be all that they can be. Michelliah has given us a wonderful and inspirational tool in her series "I AM" which is an excellent resource on how to empower girls at a young stage in life which only leads to great women for the future!

Almarie Chalmers, mother of NBA Player Mario Chalmers
Retired Educator, Author of "The Ball is in Your Court," Founder of MVC Foundation

Girls need to feel empowered and know they have the power to make their own choices in life – this book embraces all that being a girl entails!

Patricia D. Yackel
Retired Principal and Educator

What an amazing book for girls of all ages to read.

As intended, this book will build character, eliminate identity crisis, help girls embrace who they are, encourage acceptance, equip girls for adulthood and instill core values.

It is colorful, positive and provides essential tips concerning relationships, as well as a female's journey through elementary, middle school, high school, college and ultimately, womanhood.

I encourage every mom, dad, and grandparent to purchase one for their daughter and every girl they know. It will be money well spent.

I am confident that the girls will enjoy reading it as much as I have, and as much as the author, Michelliah McCraney, did in writing it.

Alena King Lawson
Retired Lieutenant, Gainesville Police Department
Chief Investigator, Public Defender's Office

To: Marquitta, Taylor, and D'Shari

To: My host of nieces

To: Every girl I've mentored and taught me in return.

From girlhood to womanhood, may your journey
I be filled with smiles, fun memories, and interesting
moments!

Dear Reader,

Embrace being a GIRL.

Guard your heart.
Proverb 4:23

Set goals and accomplish them.

Become who and what you aspire to be.

Don't Rush!

Take baby steps forward into woman-adulthood.

Have Fun! Laugh! Celebrate!

But know that it's ok to cry when needed.

Embrace moments and memories.

Be good to yourself, as well as others.

First things, first Girls:

Scratch my back

tickle my toes

wiggle my feet

squeeze my cheeks

and make me squeek

because we're about to take a peek.

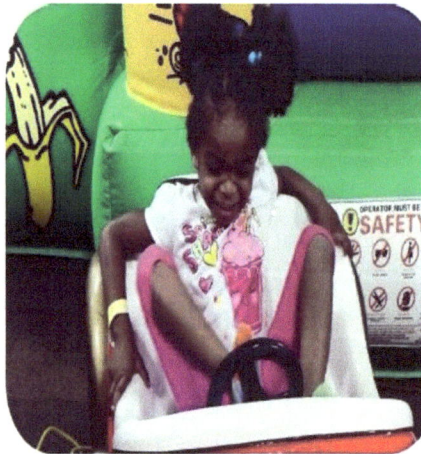

"I AM!"
A Girl

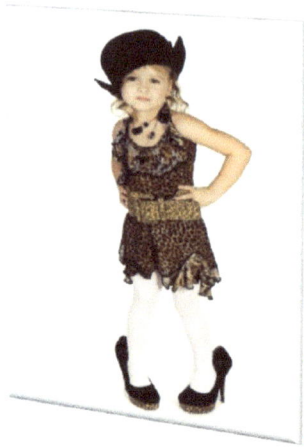

Little girls like to dress up, and pretend to be all grown up like their mothers or older siblings. They like to put on high-heeled shoes that are twice their size, accessories, and sometimes even lipstick or makeup to make them feel or look like big girls.

And because girls like to mimic those who they admire or look up to, most pre-school age girls choose to play in the house area at center time for the opportunity to role play with their peers. They do things like put their hands on their hips and pretend to be the adult.

Lots of young girls like playing with baby dolls and playing house. And because girls are natural caregivers, many girls desire to be mothers when they grow up and are old enough to be. Playing with baby dolls allows us girls to role play (model after our mothers or guardians), and with our make believe babies, we express our caring nature and motherly instinct.

Growing up, I and my sisters had **baby dolls**, **paper dolls** and **doll heads**. I can especially remember having a baby doll called "Baby Alive." She talked, crawled, and moved her mouth. Whenever I gave her water, she would even wet her diaper. Like a real mommy, I would change her diaper, feed, dress and comb her hair. I would even read her a story and rock her to sleep.

Some **G**irls like to chew gum and blow bubbles. Girls

like to pop the gum as they chew and see how big of a
bubble they can blow. I can remember as a little girl when
we would have bubble-blowing contests...

Play hop scotch, Pat-A-Cake, jump rope, hula-hoop; swing, and cheer.

All of these are and always will be some of my favorite games. But when it come to pat-a-cake and cheering, I just love moving my hands and my feet to those rhyming words and rythmic beats, while stumping my feet.

I remember a cheer called "I Got IT! It went a little something like this, "I Got It! Got What? I Got IT! Got What? I got that P. O. W. E. R. I Got that Girl Power! Get it! Aww get it, I got it! I got it! I got it! Get it! Aww get it, I got it! I got it! I got it!"

Maybe you and your friends can do this cheer together.

Now-a-days Girls of all-ages like to take **pictures.**

Silly pictures, funny pictures, cute pictures, selfies, and lots and lots of pictures!

Girls who are old enough to have a phone or a Face book, Twitter, Snap Chat, or Instagram page like texting and sharing those pictures with friends.

And though this is fun, and what everyone's doing these days, it is important for us girls to be careful of what we post (share) on those pages.

Accepting the wrong friends, giving access to unfamiliar people, and providing too much information like where you are, your next stop or move, or who you are with can be dangerous.

Posting pictures that reveal parts of your body or making videos of you and your friends moving your bodies in a provocative (inviting) way can also be dangerous.

As tempting and popular as social media is, using a fictitious (fake) name to create a page so you cannot be identified by your parent or guardian is not a smart thing to do.

Think about it. You may be able to hide it from them for a little while before they eventually find out you have this page, but what about all the other unfamiliar or bad people you may be exposing yourself to as a minor (child)?

As ladies we must take into consideration that perverts are everywhere, including social media. Therefore, we should not mimic what we see everyone else doing.

I Am! A GIRL

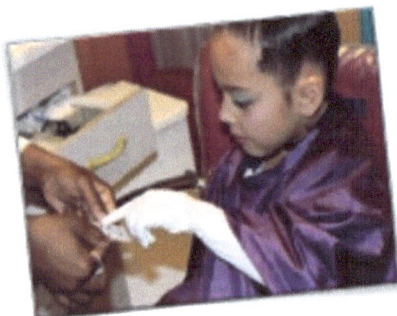

Girls like to go to the spa, hair salon, or

nail shop and get their hair, feet, nails, face, and
eyebrows done.
These are just some of the things that make them
feel good. Many find it relaxing, while others like to think
of it as a treat or how they pamper themselves.
For me and my girlfriends, it is girl time and
FUN, FUN, FUN!

Girls like to shop.

They like to shop for clothing, shoes, purses, accessories, cosmetics (beauty products), and so much more. To find what they are looking for, they'll go from store to store. Shopping is a hobby that many girls adore.

Another type of shopping that both little and big girls often do together, but consider it to be more like a chore, is shopping for food and cleaning products at the local grocery or multi-purpose department stores like Publix, Wal-Mart or Target. Although, some do prefer the farmers market or health food store.

Girls like boys

and will most likely be the first to admit liking a boy or having a crush on a boy to her girl friends. Usually once the cat is out of the bag (her friends know), he is soon to find out.

Crushes are normal and usually happen at least once or twice between elementary and middle school. Whenever a girl likes a boy, she becomes nervous, clumsy, excited, playful or even shy when she sees him or is around him. And don't be surprised if a few notes start to pass during class or she takes the time to write him a letter because its easier to say what she wants that way, instead of face to face.

And because she wants him to notice her, she goes out of the way to look her best or to be within his eyesight each and every day.

Liking boys is normal, for, it was designed by God for girls and boys and men and women to have an interest in one another. Yet, it is appropriate for the boy (man) to pursue (come after) us girls (ladies) and not the opposite (girls going after boys).

I AM! A GIRL

When it comes to Girls and high school, for most girls, it's all about the Flags, Batons, and Pom Poms.

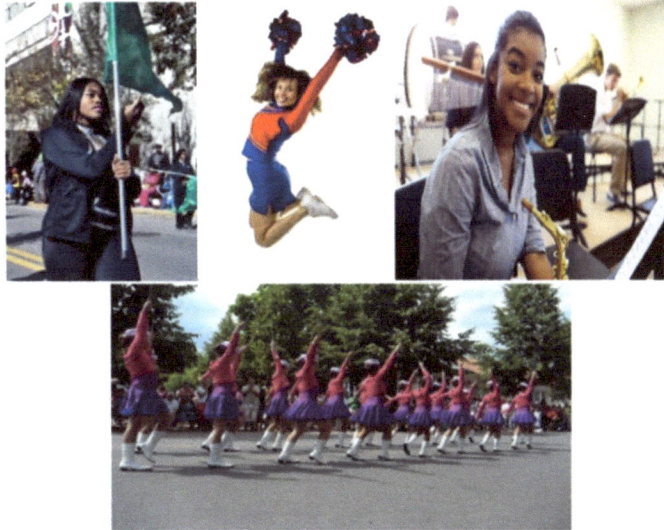

By the time most girls reach high school, they are ready to explore and try new things. High school offers all kinds of sports, clubs, activities and cool things.

In high school, many girls are known to be a large and popular part of the band. Although some play instruments, it is most popular for girls to try out to become a flaggette, cheer leader, or majorette.

While all of them have their own dance routine, special movements or presentations, the flaggettes use flags, the cheer-leaders use pom poms, and the majorettes dance and twirl the baton. For some girls, making the squad is a big deal.

But for girls who has their heart set on going to college, making the squad, graduating from high school and receiving a high school diploma will be a great accomplishment, but not enough.

These **girls** will want to pursue an associate, bachelor or even masters degree from a university or college. And if she hasn't already explored the ideal of becoming a

Member of a **S**orority, most likely she will.

Such membership offers girls an opportunity to be a part of a SISTERHOOD.

Every sorority has a set of standards that one must meet. And all of them engage in community service and help provide scholarships for high school girls.

In order to become a member of a sorority, there is usually a series of events that a girl must go through or certain qualifications she must meet. This usually determines whether or not she will be inducted (accepted) by the group.

Becoming a part of a sorority is a popular way in college for girls to make friends and interact with others. Most girls appreciate the association and leadership, but many become a member because of the organization's meaning.

MEMBERSHIP DUES are sometimes associated with being a member of a sorority. This means paying a set amount of money at a specific time.

Lastly, it is an avenue for girls to build relationships and link up with other like-minded girls at social, as well as professional gatherings and fun-filled events that may impact their future.

After all,

Girls are SISTERS. Sisters play with each other, laugh, cry, and celebrate one another. Sisters pray, shop, and hang out together.
Sisters sometime cover and take the blame for one another or tattle-tale to get the other in trouble.
Sisters sometimes argue, fuss and fight.
Call each other names and say not so nice things.
This is normal for girls that are sisters, just as it is for any other human beings with emotions and feelings.
But, because they love and trust one another, they share their deepest fears and most cherished secrets. They help and comfort one another in hard times, in hours of bereavement (mourning the loss of a loved one), or when one is sick or in pain.

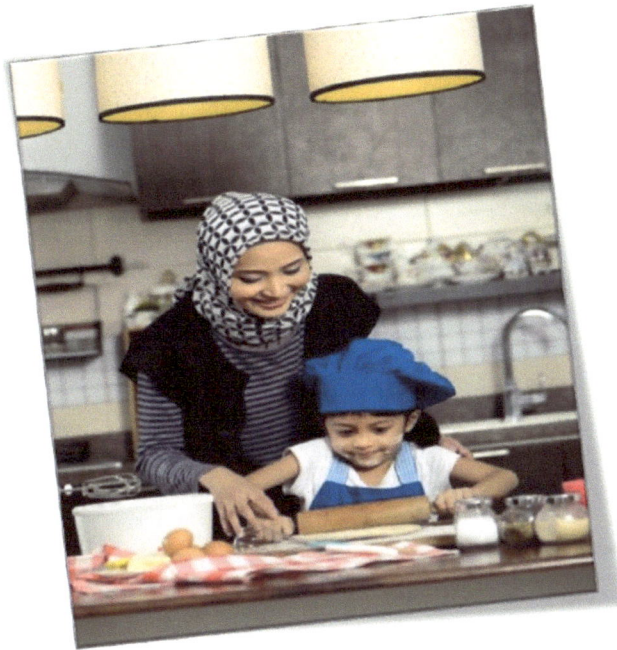

Girls are creative. Some like to cook while others like to bake. But both little and big girls enjoy sharing their ideas and recipes. Cooking is just one aspect of their creativity.

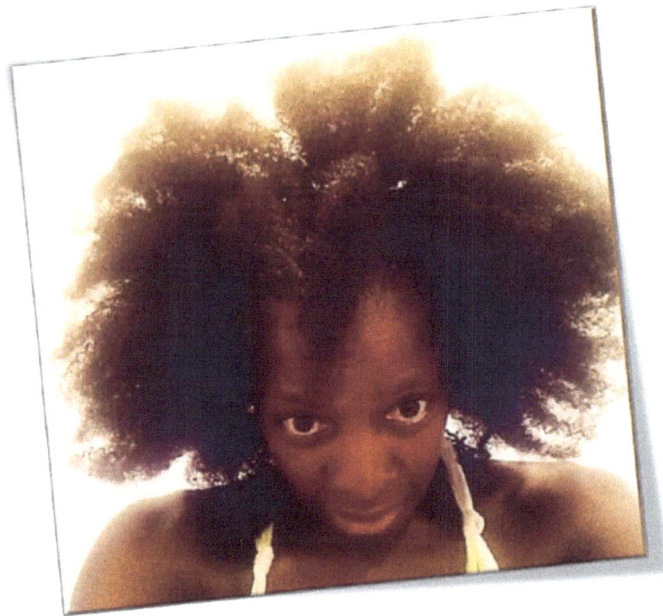

Girls have "bad hair" days and "no make-up" days.

And because they can relate, this allows them to come to each other's aid. Sisterhood or no sisterhood, many girls of age have come to realize that it is during this time that their natural beauty shines.

But don't get it twisted...

Girls are STYLISH,

FASHIONABLE, and quite ATTRACTIVE.

Girls like VARIETY. Most girls love clothing and shoes, so much so that she will not argue that she hogs up most, if not all of the closet space. And though this is true for many, it is rare for a few. That RARE FEW are the girls that dress up occasionally, and don't fall into the category of being or even coming close to being FLAMBOYANT (noticeable). And though men are MESMERIZED by physical beauty, such beauty can be found in SIMPLICITY (natural, plain, or lightly accessorized to compliment outfit) as well.

I like to consider my dress code or style to be SEXY, CONSERVATIVE. For me, this means, not exposing too much, other than my arms, back, or legs, yet appealing (irresistible, charming, fascinating, attractive) to the opposite sex, but different from the rest. I desire to attract CLASSY MEN, and not TRASHY (poor in quality/lack class) MEN.

When a man sees an attractive woman he may turn his head to take a second glance, but when he recognizes a CLASS ACT, he will acknowledge her with just one word, followed by a respectable reaction. A wise woman or most elders would say, "For heaven's sake, leave a man something to look forward to. If not, there will be no reason for him to hang around."

I AM! A GIRL

Two humanly, normal things that doesn't go well with **G**irly, girls.

Belching and passing gas. The **g**irly girls femininity (girliness) finds

belching to be pretty discusting.

She hates the way belching sounds and creeps its way up and out no matter how hard she may try to stop it from happening.

But a major blooper (embarrassing moment) for all-girls, including **pritzy's** and **tom boys** is passing gas. Girls hate passing gas.

Though the two are said to be the same, in a girl's mind passing gas changes every thing. This is one norm that if every girl can make just one wish, it would be for this to go away.

Passing gas in front of her peers or in a crowd is bad enough, but in front of a boy she likes, is a major disgrace. She'll do just about anything to avoid it, but if it does and he likes her enough, he'll probably have to find her because she'll be on the next flight headed to another city, state, or continent.

Kicking herself and shouting "Ew! Ew!" She can't imagine ever looking him again in the face.

Probably Because...

Girls are like

"SUPER HEROES!"

Some are mothers, grandmothers, god mothers, step mothers, foster mothers, and even aunties.

*T*hey wake up early, make breakfast, pack lunches, help with

homework, take the children to school, and then come back home and

make dinner, too.

They run errands, make sure all the bills are paid, return videos and books

to the library, make doctors' appointments, and write out grocery lists.

They attend school meetings and squeeze a little time in for greetings. They

support charities because they believe in giving back voluntarily.

They go to work and school, and on their days off, they do a little

housekeeping, too. They take the kids to football, basketball, and

cheerleading practice.

The day is never dull; it is filled with action. From sun up to sun

down, these women are active.

Although they are sometimes described as being strict or mean,

they will protect their children from just about anything.

For them, family is a team, and together they help each other succeed and

accomplish meaningful things as well as their dreams.

Girls have CAREERS!

Careers are what you choose.

Some are TEACHERS, POLICE OFFICERS,

SINGERS, DANCERS, MODELS, ACTORS, MENTORS,

LAWYERS, JUDGES,

NURSES, DOCTORS, VETERINARIANS,

FIRE FIGHTERS, POLITICIANS, TALK SHOW HOSTS,

AND SO MUCH MORE!

Some girls know early in life what they want to be, do or become, and others have no clue. Choosing a career is a major part of preparing and planning for your future.

When you choose a career, it should be something that you can see yourself doing for most of your life. So make sure it is something you desire to do and think that you would enjoy doing.

Later, as you grow, reach high school, or consider going to college, you will choose a major (subject) that should go hand in hand with your career choice.

Remember, this is how you will earn your own money and one day take care of yourself and your responsibilities (bills, food, clothing, etc.). It will also help you to maintain the lifestyle you choose to live, such as the car you want to drive or the house and community you desire to live in.

Working before choosing a career allows you the opportunity to learn about things you have an interest in and to develop skills, knowledge, and experience that you can take with you wherever you go.

You can use those previous jobs and supervisors as referrences to apply for other or better jobs that will require some knowledge about your background and work experience.

Those jobs may also help you in the process of choosing a career. Your education and work experience will determine what positions you qualify for as well as how much a job may be willing to pay you.

Again, choose a career that you can be happy with but also that will help you to maintain your independence and become the Career Woman of your choice.

Remember, you do not have to wait until you are an adult to start thinking about a CAREER. The time is now!

And because girls have lots and lots of choices when it comes to what they can become, many

*G*irls...

*D*ream of becoming *B*rides!

*T*hey get engaged, get married, and after the wedding, they

become wives.

Wives are help-mates to their husbands, and TOGETHER, they
BECOME ONE.

They are partners on the same team and best friends for a

LIFE-TIME...

They plan, work and take vacations together because marriage is
FOREVER and EVER.

The man and the woman take vows and give each other a ring as
a symbol of their love and commitment to one another.

Again, because MARRIAGE is for ETERNITY...

it comes with great responsibility!

And though some marriages end in divorce, it was never God's
intention and that is why it breaks everyone's heart.

You see, Proverbs 18:22 in the Bible says that a man who finds a
wife, finds a treasure (a good-thing), and receives favor from the
Lord.

That is why it is hard to see marriages fall a part.

Girls...

Dream of becoming Mommies!

They get PREGNANT and have babies. They carry their babies for nine months in their wombs. Some pray, read, sing and talk to their unborn babies. For some girls, the first couple of months of pregnancy are filled with morning sickness and cravings for different types of food. Their stomachs stretch and do all types of weird things that no one can explain. Girls' bodies are uniquely designed and equipped for this.

Most girls' dreams are to wait until they get married and established with a good job or education before they get pregnant.

This is good because then they are able to provide better for their babies and give them a home with a mommy and a daddy prayerfully filled with lots and lots of love.

Some **G**irls...

Enjoy being "**H**OMEMAKERS!"

Homemakers are STAY-AT-HOME MOMS and WIVES.

They take care of the home while everyone is gone. They clean the house from top to bottom.

They make the beds, sweep, mop, cook, sew, wash dishes, do the laundry, iron, and fold the clothes. They are known to throw away things that look, smell, or appear to be old.

They are available when the children wake up fevering or coughing with a cold, or their husband's yelling, "Honey I cannot find my favorite tie, or matching shoe," and now everything is spinning out of control.

And because it is her task to keep her home whole, she manages to find and give everybody what they need. Then out the door everybody goes.

while other *G*irls…

*A*Spire to become

"*E*NTREPRENEURS!"

These are the girls that do not work for a "company" or anyone else. They are either "self-employed or own their own businesses." This means that they work independently to earn money. They use their own ideas, talents, and gifts to be creative for the type of service they wish to provide to others.

"DADDY'S LITTLE

GIRL."

Though every girl has a dad, unfortunately, not every girl's dad is in her life.

Some know who their dad is and others have no clue.

Some have granddads, step dads, or uncles, and they are cool for dads too.

But every girl has A FATHER IN HEAVEN and He loves YOU!

Being pink (a girl) is a piece of cake, especially when we're talking strawberry shortcake.

I guess this is where I'm supposed to say, "See you later or until you and I meet again."

Banana split, full split, or half split.

Yes! It is true, no matter how old or young…

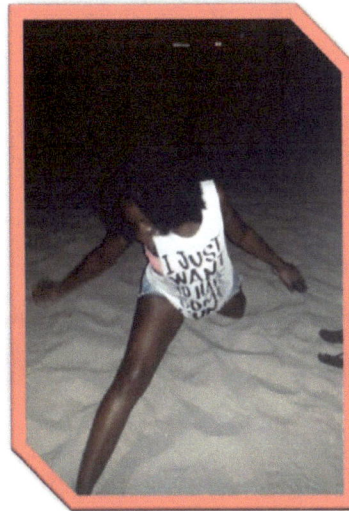

GIRLS JUST WANT TO HAVE FUN!

The End!

I AM! Michelliah McCraney, the author of this book.

"I Am! A grown up, little girl that like to have FUN!"
And it was soooooo much fun writing this book,
to educate, equip and empower YOU!

Michelliah McCraney

Was born and raised in South Florida, the place in which she avidly mentors youth and coaches parents. She is a parent educator, mother, grandmother, and inspirational speaker with a focus on girls, youth and families. To learn more about the author and her work, visit michelliah.com